The Skills Advantage

Identifying Your Skills for School, Work, and Life

by
J. Michael Farr
&
Susan Christophersen

from

jist the job search people

Publisher: J. Michael Farr
Project Director: Spring Dawn Reader
Editor: Sara Adams
Cover Design: Dean Johnson Design Group
Illustration Selection and Arrangement: Mike Kreffel
Interior Design: Spring Dawn Reader
Composition/Layout: Carolyn J. Newland

Career & Life Skills Series: The Skills Advantage—*Identifying Your Skills for School, Work, and Life*

©1994, **JIST Works, Inc.**, Indianapolis, IN

99 98 97   9 8 7 6 5 4

Send all inquiries to:

JIST Works, Inc.
720 North Park Avenue
Indianapolis, IN 46202-3431
Phone: **(317) 264-3720** • FAX: **(317) 264-3709**

ISBN: 1-56370-093-X

Table of Contents

Chapter Four—Creating a Skills Data Base 35

Chapter Five—Planning on How to Best Use Your Skills 47

Chapter One

Taking Control of Your Life

The goals of this chapter are:

- ◆ *To understand what it means to accept responsibility.*
- ◆ *To discover why taking responsibility helps you live a more satisfying life.*
- ◆ *To analyze how you spend your time.*

Are You Doing What Is Important to You?

Later in this book, you will learn how to identify your key skills. These are skills that you are particularly good at or like to use. You will learn how to use your skills to help you succeed in school, in work, or in life.

But before you learn more about your skills, you should first think about what is most important in your life. You should also think about how you want to spend your time. That is what this chapter is about. Later, you can decide how to apply your key skills to areas where you want to spend most of your time.

This Is Your Life

Ask yourself these questions:

1. Whose life are you living?
2. Whose life **should** you be living?
3. Whose life do you want to be living?

Life is full of questions. The questions present choices. It's up to you to make the choices that work best for you.

> *The choices you make determine the quality of your life.*

No one knows you better than you know yourself. No one ever will. When it comes to your life, YOU are the expert.

Now ask yourself these questions:

1. How can I create the best life possible for myself?
2. Do I feel I'm totally in control of my life?

Consider these questions and what they mean carefully. Give them a lot of thought. They are some of the most important questions you will ever have to answer.

> *You take control of your life by taking responsibility for your life.*

↪ **Think About It**

■ In the following spaces, write down some ideas about what you think it means to be totally in control of your life.

_____

_____

_____

_____

_____

_____

_____

_____

_____

_____

_____

_____

_____

_____

_____

_____

_____

_____

What Does It Mean to Take Responsibility?

Taking responsibility means that you:

■ Don't blame anyone else for what happens to you.

■ Don't try to control anyone else.

■ Do take credit for what you do right.

■ Do admit that you make mistakes.

■ Do promise to learn from every mistake.

■ Do consider the consequences of your actions before you act.

> *It's better to make a new mistake than to keep making the old one.*

Learning to take responsibility for yourself is very hard. Everyone has problems with this at one time or another. Many people, even many adults, never quite learn to be completely responsible. It is difficult to master responsibility. But it is well worth the effort. In the next chapter you'll see that accepting responsibility is a "key" skill—one that helps you get along in life.

Accepting Responsibility Is Good for You

When you accept responsibility for your life, you gain power. You are no longer under anyone else's control. Your thoughts are your own. Your feelings are your own. You own yourself.

When you blame other people for what happens to you or for how you feel, you lose power. You give it away. You're saying to those people, "You have more power over how I feel than I do. You have more power over what I think, and what happens to me, than I do." What this means is that those people have control over you. Do you want other people to control your life? Or do you want to take control for yourself?

Accepting full responsibility gives you the power to be in control of your own life. It frees you to make choices. It lets you take the opportunities to get what you need and want in your life—even if that means taking risks.

You might feel afraid of making choices and taking risks. Everyone does. But it's part of taking control. And taking control is one of the keys to living a truly satisfying life.

☞ Think About It

■ In the following spaces, list the areas in your life where you want more control. It can be anything from finding the time to study more, to learning a new job skill, to eating the right foods.

_____   _____

_____   _____

_____   _____

_____   _____

_____   _____

_____   _____

_____   _____

_____   _____

_____   _____

_____   _____

■ Now review your list. Are you are willing to accept total responsibility for all these areas? Place a checkmark beside the ones that you are.

Your Time: Do You Spend It Well?

Are you stealing from yourself? Time is like money. If you use it all up on things that aren't very important, you are cheating yourself. You don't gain anything of value. You may have a lot of things, but they don't mean much if you don't have the time to enjoy them, or if they're keeping you from doing something really important. Time is precious. Wasting your time is like stealing one of your most valuable possessions.

The Time-Tracking Chart

During the next seven days, keep a record of how you spend your time. Use the "Time-Tracking Chart" on the next pages to see how you actually spend your time.

DIRECTIONS: In the "Activity" column, you will write down each activity you do that day. For example, "Ate breakfast," "Went shopping," "Went to work." In the "Time" column, write down when you started the activity and when you stopped, as in "6:30–6:45 a.m.," "9:00–11:00 a.m.," and so on. In the "Benefits to Me or Others" column, write down how this activity has helped you or someone else. For example, "Learned new computer program," "Earned money for clothes," "I'm closer to my goal of making better grades," "I was tired and needed this break," "Helped a friend do homework," and "Jogging keeps me in shape."

Time-Tracking Chart

Activity	Time	Benefits to Me or Others
Monday		
Tuesday		
Wednesday		
Thursday		

Time-Tracking Chart

Activity	Time	Benefits to Me or Others
Friday		
Saturday		
Sunday		

🏳 **Think About It**

■ After you tracked your time for a week, what did you learn about yourself? How do you spend most of your time? Add your time spent doing the same activity throughout the week. In the left column below, list the 5 activities in which you spent most of your time. In the right column, list the 5 activities you enjoyed doing the most. Compare the columns.

How I Spent Most of My Time	**What I Enjoyed Doing Most**
1. _____	1. _____
2. _____	2. _____
3. _____	3. _____
4. _____	4. _____
5. _____	5. _____

■ Are you spending enough time on the things that are important to you? How could you spend more time on the things that matter the most to you? Write your notes on what you learned below.

_____

_____

_____

_____

_____

_____

_____

_____

_____

_____

_____

_____

_____

_____

_____

✓ **Checkpoint**

■ After completing this chapter, answer these questions. They will help you review what you learned. Your answers will also help you decide how you can use what you just learned.

1. How can you take control of your life?

   _____

   _____

   _____

   _____

   _____

   _____

2. Why is it good for you to take responsibility for yourself?

   _____

   _____

   _____

   _____

   _____

   _____

3. How do taking responsibility for yourself and how you use your time relate with each other?

   _____

   _____

   _____

   _____

   _____

   _____

4. How can you spend more time doing what you want to do and what you like to do?

   _____

   _____

   _____

   _____

   _____

   _____

ACTIVITY: Developing Awareness of Time and Responsibility

■ **INDIVIDUAL ACTIVITY:** Think of someone you know who complains often about "how life is treating" him or her. Then write answers to the questions below. (This exercise is not meant to criticize or pass judgment on someone. But you can learn from looking at the behavior of others.)

1. Does this person seem happy? Why or why not?

_____

_____

_____

_____

_____

_____

2. Does this person blame other people for his or her situation in life? If so, what do you think of this?

_____

_____

_____

_____

_____

_____

3. Does this person take responsibility for his or her life? If so, how? If not, what makes you think this way?

_____

_____

_____

_____

_____

_____

■ **GROUP ACTIVITY:** Discuss ways to spend time productively. Earning money, being with friends or family, and learning something new are some examples. How do these activities help you? What are some more examples and how can they help you?

Chapter Two

What Are Skills?

The goals of this chapter are:

- ◆ To understand what skills are.
- ◆ To see why knowing your skills can help you in your learning, career, and life.
- ◆ To learn about the kinds of skills that are most important to you.

Defining Skills

A skill is something you can do. Reading, writing, and cooking a meal are examples of skills. A skill can also be part of your personality. You might be skillful at getting along with others or good at organizing things.

Most activities require sets of skills that can be broken down into "smaller" skills. If you can learn to do the smaller skills, the whole activity becomes much easier to master.

Skills Breakdown

Driving a car is just one example of using many sets of skills in order to do an activity. Here are just some of the skills needed to drive a car:

- reading road signs
- eye-hand coordination
- parallel parking
- remembering traffic laws
- applying the brakes and accelerating correctly in different situations
- understanding road maps and directions

- concentrating
- knowing how to back up
- avoiding dangerous situations
- knowing how to operate all controls
- interpreting infgormation from rearview mirrors

As you can see, it takes many skills to drive a car. You may not realize how many skills you already have. Most people have hundreds of skills. You probably do, too. Does that surprise you? Like most people, you have probably developed some skills much more than others.

☞ Think About It

■ Think about all the skills you use now. They can be skills you use in school, at work, at home, or elsewhere. Write them in the spaces below. You can list the same skill in more than one column.

School Skills	Work Skills	Leisure Skills
_____	_____	_____
_____	_____	_____
_____	_____	_____
_____	_____	_____
_____	_____	_____
_____	_____	_____
_____	_____	_____
_____	_____	_____
_____	_____	_____
_____	_____	_____
_____	_____	_____
_____	_____	_____
_____	_____	_____
_____	_____	_____
_____	_____	_____
_____	_____	_____
_____	_____	_____

Which of these skills are you best at using? Place a checkmark next to the skills you listed that you think you are best at. Which ones do you especially like to use? Place a double checkmark next to these skills. The skills with the most checkmarks would be your best skills. However, you have many, many more skills, even if you haven't developed them yet.

Your best skills are the ones you do well and enjoy using.

Why Do You Need to Know Your Skills?

The things that you are good at and the things that you enjoy doing are an important part of who you are. Throughout our lives—in school, in work, and in our free or leisure time—our skills become a central part of our lives.

That is why we enjoy some school classes more than others. Whatever work we choose, we are happiest when we do work that is satisfying and meaningful to us. It may be unpaid work such as raising children, or part-time work, or work that we have been trained and educated to do. And the same is true for how we spend our leisure time—we are happiest when spending time in a satisfying and meaningful way to us.

✍ **Think About It**

■ What school classes have you enjoyed the most?

_____

_____

_____

_____

_____

_____

_____

_____

■ What work do you enjoy doing so much that you would do it for free?

_____

_____

_____

_____

_____

_____

_____

_____

_____

■ What things do you most like to do in your leisure time?

_____

_____

_____

_____

_____

_____

_____

_____

Knowing Your Skills Helps You Choose Activities That Are Right for You

Listed below are several reasons why you need to know your skills:

- So you can choose activities that you enjoy and will best meet your needs.
- So you can best plan for your additional learning or leisure needs.
- So you can use your best skills to get a satisfying job.

Let's look at these reasons in more detail.

Choosing Activities That You Enjoy and Will Best Meet Your Needs

If you know what you are good at and enjoy doing, you are much more likely to do those activities. Satisfaction in any of your life activities is directly related to using skills that you enjoy using. So it makes sense to know what those skills are.

Planning for Your Additional Learning or Leisure Needs

Knowing in advance the things that you are best at will help you plan your learning and leisure activities. For example, you may want to get additional education in order to gain the skills you need to get a certain type of job you want. Or you can plan your free time to do the things you enjoy that you are not able to do elsewhere.

Using Your Best Skills to Get a Satisfying Job

Knowing your skills is very important in deciding on what type of job to look for. Whenever you go to a job interview, the most important question that you'll have to answer is, "Why should I hire you?" Any employer is going to expect you to be able to answer that question.

You can't just say, "Because I'm a nice person," or "Because I really need to make some money." You'll have to convince an employer that you have the skills to do the job.

Many job applicants don't know how to do that. They don't know how to talk about their skills or their good worker traits.

> *You have a better chance of being hired if you can communicate your skills to an employer.*

Even though you have hundreds of skills, some will be more important to an employer than others. And some will be far more important to you as you decide what sort of job you want.

In the next section, you will learn about three major types of skills. This will help you prepare to use your best skills in planning your education, your career, your leisure time, and your life.

The Skills Triangle

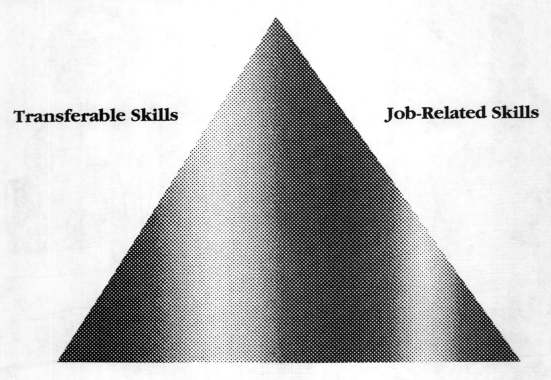

Transferable Skills   **Job-Related Skills**

Self-Management Skills

"The Skills Triangle" is a system that groups your skills into three major types. We will look at these types one by one.

Adaptive Skills or Personality Traits

These are skills you use every day to survive and get along. They might be skills you have learned, or they could be part of your basic personality. Adaptive skills are also called self-management skills. They help you get along in different situations. Some examples of adaptive skills are:

- Honesty
- An enthusiastic attitude
- The ability to follow instructions

Transferable Skills

These are general skills that can "transfer" from job to job. For example, good communication skills are useful in many different jobs. Transferable skills are very important to employers. Some examples of transferable skills are:

- Being able to manage people
- The ability to solve problems
- Keeping track of money

Job-Related Skills

These are skills a person must know to do a specific job or type of job. The job can't be done without these skills. For example:

- An auto mechanic must know how to tune engines and repair brakes.
- A teacher must be able to present information in a way that students can understand.

- A secretary must be able to type and communicate well.

Job-related skills are important, but they are not the most important thing that an employer considers. Often an employer will be willing to train an employee to learn the necessary job-related skills. The employee must have the right adaptive and transferable skills to get the job, but the job-related skills can sometimes be learned on the job.

The exercise that follows shows why transferable and adaptive skills can get you hired for a job, even if you don't have all the job-related skills right now.

☞ Think About It

Imagine that you are the manager of a local delivery company. You have one job opening and two job applicants to choose from. You are looking over your notes about each applicant. Here are your notes:

Applicant #1: Has experience as a delivery truck driver. Checked with previous employer. Was late for work fairly often. Missed some deliveries. Good driving record. Couldn't find location of delivery on several occasions, and left customers without supplies. Doesn't seem real motivated.

Applicant #2: No experience on this type of job. Previous employer says applicant hardly ever missed a day of work, was always on time, and dependable. Very enthusiastic. Seems eager to learn.

■ Which applicant would you hire? In the spaces that follow explain why.

_____

_____

_____

_____

_____

_____

_____

_____

_____

_____

_____

_____

_____

_____

_____

_____

_____

_____

_____

_____

Chances are, an employer will choose the same person for the same reasons you did. In the next chapter, you'll work with worksheets to identify your best skills of the three types in "The Skills Triangle."

✓ **Checkpoint**

■ After completing this chapter, answer these questions. They will help you review what you just learned.

1. What are skills? Give some examples of your skills.

_____

_____

_____

_____

_____

_____

2. How can knowing your skills help you find the job you want?

_____

_____

_____

_____

_____

_____

3. Explain what the three types of skills are and tell which ones are most important to an employer.

_____

_____

_____

_____

_____

_____

4. How can knowing your skills actually save you time?

_____

_____

_____

_____

_____

_____

ACTIVITY: Developing Your Skills Awareness

■ **INDIVIDUAL ACTIVITY:** Think of a job that might interest you. Find out everything you can about what skills are involved in doing that job. You can do this by talking to someone you know who does this job. You can also go to the library and ask for a book on career information. Two books we recommend are *Exploring Careers* and the *Occupational Outlook Handbook.* After you have gathered information about the skills needed, answer these questions:

1. What job-related skills do you already have for this job?

_____
_____
_____
_____
_____

2. What job-related skills would you have to learn?

_____
_____
_____
_____
_____

3. What transferable skills do you already have for this job?

_____
_____
_____
_____
_____

4. What adaptive skills do you already have for this job?

_____
_____
_____
_____
_____

■ **GROUP ACTIVITY:** Discuss jobs that members of the group or class have done. These can be paid or unpaid, part-time or otherwise. Discuss the skills that these jobs require, and how these skills are acquired.

Chapter Three

Identifying Your Adaptive and Transferable Skills

The goals of this chapter are:

◆ *To identify your skills.*

◆ *To understand how you can use your skills in learning, career, leisure, and life planning.*

◆ *To begin learning how to communicate those skills.*

Your Adaptive and Transferable Skills

In chapter 2, you learned about three types of skills. They are adaptive skills/personality traits, transferable skills, and job-related skills. When you identify your best skills in each of these groups, you can:

■ Make good decisions about your learning, career, and leisure options.

■ Answer the most important question an employer will ask: "Why should I hire you?"

Your Adaptive Skills

■ On the following lines, list three things about you that help you get along in life. They could be your best traits. Take your time. Think about how you adapt to different situations.

1. _____

2. _____

3. _____

These three traits are some of the most important things you need to know about yourself. They define the way you see yourself and what you have to offer others.

Many people think these skills or traits are not important enough to talk about, but they are. In a job interview, for example, mentioning these traits may get you hired over someone who actually has more experience than you do.

Adaptive Skills Worksheet

The worksheet that follows contains a list of adaptive skills. The first group of skills are the most important ones. Many employers will not hire an applicant who does not have these skills. The second group of skills are important ones for many jobs.

> **Directions:** *Look over the list and put a checkmark beside any skill that you feel you have now. In the "Want to Improve" column, put a checkmark beside any skill that you feel you need to improve. (Later in this book we will go over ways to develop and improve your skills.)*
>
> *At the end of the worksheet, you can add other skills that you feel you have now or want to improve that are not listed here.*

ADAPTIVE SKILLS WORKSHEET		
Basic Adaptive Skills (the minimum)		
Skill	**Have Now**	**Want to Improve**
Good attendance		
Honest		
Arriving on time		
Following instructions		
Meeting deadlines		
Hard-working		
Getting along with others		
Other Adaptive Skills		
Skill	**Have Now**	**Want to Improve**
Ambition		
Patience		
Flexibility		
Maturity		
Assertiveness		
Dependability		
Learning quickly		
Completing assignments		
Sincerity		
Motivation		
Problem Solving		
Friendliness		

ADAPTIVE SKILLS WORKSHEET

Other Adaptive Skills

Skill	Have Now	Want to Improve
Sense of humor		
Leadership		
Physical stamina		
Enthusiasm		
Good sense of direction		
Persistence		
Self-motivating		
Accepting responsibility		
Results-oriented		
Willing to ask questions		
Pride in doing a good job		
Willing to learn		
Creativity		

More Adaptive Skills (add your own)

Skill	Have Now	Want to Improve

Your Top Adaptive Skills

■ Review your list of adaptive skills. Then, in the spaces below, list the three adaptive skills that you feel are most important for an employer to know about you.

1. _____

2. _____

3. _____

■ Now list the three adaptive skills that you feel are the most important ones for you to work on improving. (Keep these in mind for later. We'll work on improving skills in a later chapter.)

1. _____

2. _____

3. _____

Your Transferable Skills

■ On the three lines below, list what you think are your top transferable skills. Remember, these are the skills that you can take with you from job to job. It is important for you to know these skills so you can share them with a potential employer.

1. _____

2. _____

3. _____

There are hundreds of transferable skills. The worksheet that follows includes the ones that are most important to employers. Complete the next section to see if the skills you listed are included on the worksheet.

Transferable Skills Worksheet

The skills on this worksheet are organized into clusters. This is to help you identify major types of jobs that will suit you best.

> **DIRECTIONS:** *Read the list and put a checkmark beside each skill that you feel you are strong in. Then go through the list again and put another checkmark in the "Use in Next Job" column if you think you want to use that skill in your next job.*
>
> *Note: The "key" skills at the beginning of the worksheet are used in jobs that tend to pay more. If you have any of these skills, you will want to emphasize them to possible employers.*

TRANSFERABLE SKILLS WORKSHEET

Key Transferable Skills

Skill	Already Strong	Use in Next Job
Meeting deadlines		
Planning		
Public speaking		
Budgeting and money management		
Supervising others		
Instructing others		
Accepting responsibility		
Managing people		
Meeting the public		
Organizing projects		
Taking risks		
Self-controlling		
Self-motivating		
Detail-oriented		
Explaining things to others		
Problem solving		
Good writing skills		
Good math skills		

Other Transferable Skills: Working with Things

Skill	Already Strong	Use in Next Job
Using my hands		

TRANSFERABLE SKILLS WORKSHEET

Other Transferable Skills: Working with Things

Skill	Already Strong	Use in Next Job
Assembling things		
Building things		
Constructing, repairing buildings		
Making things		
Observing, inspecting things		
Driving or operating vehicles		
Operating tools and machinery		
Using complex equipment		

Other Transferable Skills: Working with Data

Skill	Already Strong	Use in Next Job
Analyzing data, facts		
Auditing records		
Investigating		
Locating answers, information		
Calculating, computing		
Classifying data		
Counting		
Researching		
Observing		

Other Transferable Skills: Working with People

Skill	Already Strong	Use in Next Job
Patient		
Sensitive		
Social		
Tactful		
Teaching		
Interviewing others		
Listening		
Tolerant		
Understanding		
Kind		

TRANSFERABLE SKILLS WORKSHEET

Other Transferable Skills: Working with People

Skill	Already Strong	Use in Next Job
Diplomatic		
Counseling people		
Confronting (when necessary)		
Trusting		
Can be firm		

Other Transferable Skills: Using Words, Ideas

Skill	Already Strong	Use in Next Job
Can be logical		
Speaking in public		
Designing		
Editing		
Remembering information		
Writing clearly		
Corresponding with others		
Creative		

Other Transferable Skills: Using Leadership Ability

Skill	Already Strong	Use in Next Job
Arranging social functions		
Competitive		
Motivating people		
Can be decisive		
Running meetings		
Delegating		
Working out agreements		
Planning		

Other Transferable Skills: Using Creative, Artistic Ability

Skill	Already Strong	Use in Next Job
Dancing, body movement		
Drawing, art		
Performing, acting		

TRANSFERABLE SKILLS WORKSHEET

Other Transferable Skills: Using Creative, Artistic Ability

Skill	Already Strong	Use in Next Job
Playing instruments		
Presenting artistic ideas		
Music appreciation		
Expressive		

Other Transferable Skills: Add Your Own

Skill	Already Strong	Use in Next Job

Your Top Transferable Skills

■ Review your list of transferable skills. Then check the ones you are best in or that are most important to you. List your five best transferable skills below.

1. _____
2. _____
3. _____
4. _____
5. _____

■ Now list the five skills you most want to improve. (We'll work on improving your skills later in this book.)

1. _____
2. _____
3. _____
4. _____
5. _____

■ In the next chapter, you will create a "data base" of your experiences. This listing of experiences can be used to help you uncover even more skills, including job-related skills.

✓ **Checkpoint**

■ After completing this chapter, answer these questions. They will help you review what you just learned.

1. What are "adaptive" skills?

_____

_____

_____

_____

_____

_____

_____

2. What are "transferable" skills?

_____

_____

_____

_____

_____

_____

_____

3. Why is it so important for you to know and be able to communicate your adaptive and transferable skills?

_____

_____

_____

_____

_____

_____

_____

ACTIVITY: Practice Communicating Your Skills

■ **INDIVIDUAL ACTIVITY:** Look back at the three top adaptive skills that you listed. Think about situations in your life when you used each of those skills. Briefly describe those situations and how you used the skills. Can you support your claim that you have these skills? (This becomes very important during job interviews.)

Adaptive Skill #1 _____

How I used this skill: _____

_____

_____

_____

_____

_____

_____

Adaptive Skill #2 _____

How I used this skill: _____

_____

_____

_____

_____

_____

_____

Adaptive Skill #3 _____

How I used this skill: _____

_____

_____

_____

_____

_____

_____

■ **GROUP ACTIVITY:** Each member of the class describes one or more of his or her top five transferable skills. You should explain how you learned these skills and how you would like to use them in a future job, leisure, or learning activity.

Chapter Four

Creating a Skills Data Base

The goals of this chapter are:

◆ *To create a skills data base using your life history.*

◆ *To use your data base to support your having key skills.*

◆ *To use your data base to identify job-related skills.*

◆ *To use your data base to plan education, career, or leisure activities.*

Use Your Life Experience to Know Your Skills and Choose Work That's Right for You

In chapter 3, you used worksheets to identify your adaptive and transferable skills. These were two of the types of skills from "The Skills Triangle."

In this chapter, you will be gathering information about yourself from all the experiences that you have had. In these experiences are keys to who you are and what you have spent time and effort on. There are also keys to what you do well and what you are likely to do well in the future.

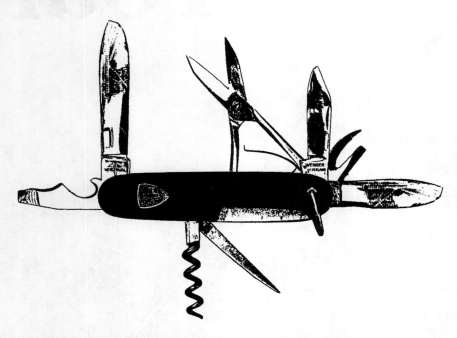

Your Skills Data Base

Completing the worksheets that follow will help you form a skills data base. With this data base you will see that many of your life experiences can support your adaptive and transferable skills. The data base can also help identify your job-related skills, the third group of skills from "The Skills Triangle." Job-related skills don't just come from jobs you have had or have been trained for. You probably have many skills that you have developed through participating in a variety of activities.

The data base you put together in this chapter will be very important to your career and life planning. It will help you:

■ Identify more skills.

■ Identify your interests and accomplishments.

■ Describe experiences that explain and support your skills.

This knowledge can be used to help you make good decisions about your career, additional education, or how you spend your leisure time. And it can help you get a good job. For example, you have a better chance of convincing an employer to hire you when you can prove your skills.

Skills Data Base Worksheet

> **DIRECTIONS:** *Complete the worksheet that follows to target the key experiences and skills you gained during your education or training.*

Education and Training

Junior High School

■ Include coursework that relates to your job interests.

Subjects Studied	Skills Acquired
_____	_____
_____	_____
_____	_____
_____	_____
_____	_____
_____	_____
_____	_____
_____	_____

■ Include any special organizations that you participated in, whether in or out of school. These might be clubs, teams, hobby groups, and so forth.

Extracurricular Activities	Skills Acquired
_____	_____
_____	_____
_____	_____
_____	_____
_____	_____
_____	_____
_____	_____

High School

■ Include coursework that relates to your job interests.

Subjects Studied	Skills Acquired
_____	_____
_____	_____
_____	_____
_____	_____
_____	_____
_____	_____
_____	_____
_____	_____
_____	_____

■ Include any special organizations that you participated in, whether in or out of school. These might be clubs, teams, hobby groups, and so forth.

Extracurricular Activities	Skills Acquired
_____	_____
_____	_____
_____	_____
_____	_____
_____	_____
_____	_____
_____	_____
_____	_____
_____	_____

After High School

■ In this section, list any education or training you had after high school. Include training you have received in the military, if any.

Subjects Studied	Skills Acquired
_____	_____
_____	_____
_____	_____
_____	_____
_____	_____
_____	_____
_____	_____
_____	_____
_____	_____

Extracurricular Activities	Skills Acquired
_____	_____
_____	_____
_____	_____
_____	_____
_____	_____
_____	_____
_____	_____

Your Top 5 Skills from Your Education and Training

Directions: *In the left column below, list your five best skills from the worksheet sections you just completed. In the right column, list the top five skills that you want to use most in your next job or career. They may or may not be the same.*

My Best Skills	**Skills I Want to Use**
1. _____	1. _____
2. _____	2. _____
3. _____	3. _____
4. _____	4. _____
5. _____	5. _____

Work History

■ For this section, you will list all the jobs you've had and what you learned from them.

Job	Skills Acquired
_____	_____
_____	_____
	_____
	_____
	_____

Job	Skills Acquired
_____	_____
_____	_____
	_____
	_____
	_____

Job	Skills Acquired
_____	_____
_____	_____
	_____
	_____
	_____

Job	Skills Acquired
_____	_____
_____	_____
	_____
	_____
	_____

Volunteer Experience

■ You don't have to have been paid for work to have valuable work experience. In this section, list any volunteer work you have done, and the skills you acquired.

Volunteer Work	**Skills Acquired**
_____	_____
_____	_____
	_____
	_____
	_____

Volunteer Work	**Skills Acquired**
_____	_____
_____	_____
	_____
	_____
	_____

Volunteer Work	**Skills Acquired**
_____	_____
_____	_____
	_____

Volunteer Work	**Skills Acquired**
_____	_____
_____	_____
	_____
	_____

Hobbies and Life Experiences

For this section, list hobbies, special interests, or special activities that have led you to develop specific skills. Take plenty of time to think and remember. As we said earlier in this book, you have many more skills than you think!

Special Activity	Skills Acquired
_____	_____
_____	_____
	_____
	_____
	_____

Special Activity	Skills Acquired
_____	_____
_____	_____
	_____
	_____
	_____

Special Activity	Skills Acquired
_____	_____
_____	_____
	_____
	_____
	_____

Special Activity	Skills Acquired
_____	_____
_____	_____
	_____
	_____
	_____

Your Top Skills

■ Now you will need to go back over the entire worksheet you just completed. Use each section to complete the lists that follow here.

Things I Do Best

1. _____
2. _____
3. _____
4. _____
5. _____

Skills I Enjoy Using Most

1. _____
2. _____
3. _____
4. _____
5. _____

Skills I Most Want to Improve

1. _____
2. _____
3. _____
4. _____
5. _____

Skills I Want to Use in My Next Job

1. _____
2. _____
3. _____
4. _____
5. _____

Congratulations! You now have a data base to help you make valuable decisions about your life and your work.

Don't worry about figuring out your entire life goals right now. People grow and change throughout their lives, and you are bound to change, too. You can't predict the future. So make the decisions that make sense now. That's the best anyone can do.

✓ **Checkpoint**

■ After completing this chapter, answer these questions. They will help you review what you just learned.

1. Were you surprised by how many skills you have acquired from your experiences? What surprised you the most?

_____

_____

_____

_____

_____

_____

_____

2. How has this data base helped you identify your skills?

_____

_____

_____

_____

_____

_____

_____

_____

3. Think of a job you might want to apply for. If you were an employer, would you hire yourself for this job? What skills do you need to work on to give you the best chance of getting the job?

_____

_____

_____

_____

_____

_____

_____

ACTIVITY: Thinking About Career Options

■ **INDIVIDUAL ACTIVITY:** Have you ever dreamed of being your own boss? This could be a real option for you. Look over your Skills Data Base, and think about the activities you enjoy the most. You might be able to combine your skills and interests to start a business of your own. Hobbies such as gardening can turn into a landscaping business, for example. If you like woodworking, you could do furniture repair and refinishing. Some of the skills required to be self-employed are:

- ■ Time management
- ■ Marketing your service or product
- ■ Self-discipline and motivation
- ■ Money management
- ■ Locating necessary supplies or equipment
- ■ Serving customers

■ Can you think of some others?

_____   _____

_____   _____

_____   _____

_____   _____

_____   _____

_____   _____

_____   _____

_____   _____

_____   _____

_____   _____

Self-employment is just one of many ways you can put your skills to work doing what you like to do. Becoming self-employed is not easy and you should carefully consider all aspects before making a decision.

If you think you are interested in self-employment, there are many good resource books such as *Mind Your Own Business* by LaVerne Ludden and Bonnie Maitlen, which will help you determine if this type of employment is right for you.

■ **GROUP ACTIVITY:** Imagine that you are all employees at the same organization. You have to work together to accomplish the goals of the organization. Discuss what skills do you need to work together. Discuss what you expect of each other as co-workers.

Chapter
Five

Planning on How to Best Use Your Skills

The goals of this chapter are:

◆ *To learn how to gather information about jobs that match your skills.*

◆ *To find out ways to develop more skills.*

◆ *To consider options for additional education or training.*

Making Your Data Base Work for You

In the last chapter you spent considerable time creating a personal data base of your skills and experiences. In this chapter you will learn how to use your data base to determine which careers would be best suited to your skills. You will also learn to identify resources for further education or training to satisfy your education, career, or liesure needs.

Using Information and Resources

Go back through chapter 3 and chapter 4 to review the skills you identified as your best skills. These are the skills that you do well and may want to use in your next job. Write them again here.

My Best Skills

Transferable	Adaptive	Job-Related
_____	_____	_____
_____	_____	_____
_____	_____	_____
_____	_____	_____
_____	_____	_____
_____	_____	_____

Jobs That Match Your Skills

There are thousands of job titles and you will need to find one that best fits your skills and interests. One way to do this is to consider groups of similar jobs. The list below provides groups of jobs organized into 12 major clusters of occupations or interest areas. Later, you can go to a library and look up the major jobs in the clusters. For now, just check the clusters of jobs that sound most interesting to you.

_____ **01 Artistic**—An interest in the creative expression of feelings or ideas.

_____ **02 Scientific**—An interest in discovering, collecting, and analyzing information about the natural world, and in applying scientific research findings to problems in medicine, and the natural sciences.

_____ **03 Plants and Animals**—An interest in working with plants and animals, usually outdoors.

_____ **04 Protective**—An interest in using authority to protect people and property.

_____ **05 Mechanical**—An interest in applying mechanical principles to practical situations by use of machines or hand tools.

_____ **06 Industrial**—An interest in repetitive, concrete, organized activities done in a factory setting.

_____ **07 Business Detail**—An interest in organized, clearly defined activities requiring accuracy and attention to details, primarily in an office setting.

_____ **08 Selling**—An interest in bringing others to a particular point of view by personal persuasion, using sales and promotional techniques.

_____ **09 Accommodating**—An interest in catering to the wishes and needs of others, usually on a one-to-one basis.

_____ **10 Humanitarian**—An interest in helping others with their mental, spiritual, social, physical, or vocational needs.

_____ **11 Leading-Influencing**—An interest in leading and influencing others by using high-level verbal or numerical abilities.

_____ **12 Physical Performing**—An interest in physical activities performed before an audience.

Gathering Information

You will probably need more information about the jobs you are interested in. You need to know about what skills are required and what training might be necessary. There may be jobs that match your skills and interests that you haven't thought of yet.

Here are some ways to find out more about the jobs that interest you.

1. Go to your public library and look up information in the following publications. (You can ask the librarian to help you find these and other resources.)

    ■ ***The Occupational Outlook Handbook:*** Published by the U.S. Department of Labor, this book provides good descriptions of the top few hundred jobs in this country. It includes information on the nature of work, average pay rates, education and training required, projections for growth, and many other details.

    ■ ***Exploring Careers:*** Written for young people, this book describes jobs in major clusters, featuring people who actually work in the jobs in some of the descriptions.

    ■ ***The Complete Guide for Occupational Exploration:*** This book lists more than 12,000 jobs in 12 major occupational clusters, 64 subgroups, and over 300 even more specific groups of similar jobs. A general description is provided for each cluster as well as typical skills and education or training required.

2. Talk to people who already have jobs in your field of interest. Contact employers and make an appointment or ask questions over the telephone about what skills and training you would need in order for them to hire you. Talk to a guidance counselor at a high school, vocational or technical school, or college or university about the type of job you are interested in.

If You Need More Training or Skills

What if you lack some of the skills or requirements for the job you want? Let's consider what your options are.

Formal Schooling

One option for gaining new skills or improving your skills is, of course, to go to school. There are many types of schools, such as colleges, universities, vocational, and technical schools. (There are reference books at your library which provide information on these schools.) If you are thinking about entering a school program, some things to consider are:

What type of school will provide the training you need?
Some options are:

- High School career training programs
- Community and junior colleges
- Four-year colleges and universities
- Vocational and technical schools

What is the reputation of the school?
Some things to check out:

- Does the school have good credentials?
- Do employers hire the schools graduates?

How will you pay for it?
Some options might be:

- Financial aid through the school or a government program
- Help from relatives or your employer
- Earning enough money by working while you go through the program
- Earn a scholarship

How can you arrange your schedule to make time for school?
You might have to:

- Change jobs or change your work schedule
- Learn to manage your time better (get up earlier or go to bed later)
- Arrange for more child care if you have children

What sacrifices you are willing to make for school?
Be prepared to:

- Give up some leisure time activities
- Give up things you might like to spend money on so that you can pay for school
- Change your lifestyle
- Set aside time for studying and homework

What is the location of the school that best suits your needs?
Can you:

- Get to class meetings regularly?
- Move if necessary?

The Military

Another option for receiving training is the Armed Forces. You can enlist in the service and learn job skills that you can use for a civilian job when you have finished your tour of duty.

You can also qualify for scholarships and other forms of financial aid for career training programs and even university degrees.

Local recruitment offices can help you find out information about career possibilities through the military. There are books such as *Military Careers* and others that are put out by the U.S. Government. These books contain information about available programs. Ask the librarian at your library to help you locate this information.

On-the-Job Training

Some jobs do not require any actual training before you take the job. You learn by doing. This kind of job training can last from a few days to several years.

Your employer might place you under the supervision of another worker, or send you to classes to train you for the job.

You might also work toward a job you want in a business or organization by starting in an entry level job. An entry level job is often low-skilled and low paying, but you can learn about the job you want to move up to. You can learn much about the organization and receive promotions if you do your work well.

Apprenticeships

An apprentice learns a trade by combining on-the-job training with classroom instruction. The program can last from one to six years.

Most programs are put on by employers, government programs, and labor unions. Bricklayers, auto mechanics, carpenters, and electricians are some of the kinds of trade workers who can learn through an apprentice program.

Self-Directed Training

■ You can improve many skills by working on your own. This is especially true of adaptive and transferable skills. Go back to chapter 3 and look over your checklists for these skills. On the lines that follow, write down again the skills that you want to improve.

_____   _____

_____   _____

_____   _____

_____   _____

_____   _____

_____   _____

■ Now choose the one that seems the most important right now. You should consider what will help you the most on the job you want when making your decision. Circle this skill or put a check mark next to it.

Use Your Outer Resources

There are many sources of help to draw on to improve the skill you have chosen. You could:

■ Ask for help from a friend or relative who is good at that skill. ("Uncle Joe, you've always been so organized. How do you do it?")

■ Find out about community programs in your area. High schools, hospitals, libraries, state universities, and many other organizations offer a wide range of adult programs on evenings and weekends. The cost is usually low.

These programs cover both personal and practical skills. A few examples are as follows:

■ Learning math skills   ■ Learning to use a computer
■ Improving reading skills   ■ Learning how to be assertive

⟋ Think About It

■ What are some other resources you might use?

_____

_____

_____

_____

_____

_____

_____

_____

_____

_____

Use Your Inner Resources

What is your most important inner resource to develop your skills? Your attitude! If you believe you will succeed, your chances of doing so increase. The opposite is also true.

If you believe you won't succeed, you probably won't. Commit yourself to a positive attitude about your goals. Put negative thoughts out of your mind, every time they come in. (This may take a lot of practice, but if you stick with it, it will become a habit.)

☞ Think About It

■ What are some other inner resources that you can draw on to improve your skills?

_____

_____

_____

_____

_____

_____

_____

_____

Make a Plan

You have a better chance of reaching any goal you set if you:

■ Make the goal very specific.

■ Gather any information you need.

■ Find someone to be supportive and give you encouragement along the way.

■ Decide on a plan to achieve the goal.

■ Keep track of your progress.

■ Stick with the plan and Do It!

Did you know that Thomas Edison failed hundreds of times before he designed a light bulb that actually worked? That's a lot of "failures!" But his basic design made electricity popular and revolutionized our world. Success is often built on a series of failures.

The worksheet that follows can help you make a plan to work on the skill you've decided to improve.

Goal Planning

♦ *Goal:* _____

(Be specific. For example, "I will know how to type by June 1, 199X.)

Information I Will Gather	**Do It By**
_____	_____
_____	_____
_____	_____
_____	_____
_____	_____
_____	_____
_____	_____

People I Need to Talk To	**Do It By**
_____	_____
_____	_____
_____	_____
_____	_____
_____	_____
_____	_____
_____	_____

What I Need to Do How I Will Do It	**Do It By**
_____	_____
_____	_____
_____	_____
_____	_____
_____	_____

Days and Times I Will Study or Practice This Skill

Day	Skill	Time
Monday		
Tuesday		
Wednesday		
Thursday		
Friday		
Saturday		
Sunday		

Measure Your Progress

When you were a child, how did you know you were growing? Maybe someone marked your height on the wall, and each time the mark was higher than the last time. Or maybe you noticed that you could reach the faucet in the sink without using a stool.

It helps to see real results. Keeping track of your progress keeps you motivated.

Some ways to keep track of your progress are:

- Buy a calendar to use only for your progress record-keeping.

- Keep a journal.

- Use index cards and keep them organized.

- Use a tape recorder as a spoken journal. Start each new entry with the date, and tell what you accomplished, how you did it, and how you feel about it. Talk about obstacles and how you will or how you did handle them.

✓ **Checkpoint**

■ After completing this chapter, answer these questions. They will help you review what you just learned.

1. What are some ways to find out information about jobs?

_____

_____

_____

_____

_____

_____

_____

2. Are failures good or bad? Why?

_____

_____

_____

_____

_____

_____

3. What can you learn from risking failure?

_____

_____

_____

_____

_____

_____

4. How does tracking your progress help you improve your skills?

_____

_____

_____

_____

_____

_____

ACTIVITY: Focus on Goals and Strategies

■ **INDIVIDUAL ACTIVITY:** Try to imagine your life 10 years from now. What kind of person do you want to be? Where do you want to be living? How would you like friends, family, and co-workers to describe you? Write your answers in the spaces below.

_____

_____

_____

_____

_____

_____

_____

_____

_____

■ **GROUP ACTIVITY:** Discuss the obstacles to mastering a new skill. Suggest positive ways to deal with obstacles. Some examples are given below.

Obstacle	**What to Do About It**
■ Fear of failure	■ Remember Edison's light bulb!
■ Lack of motivation	■ Use your goals to get you motivated.
■ Schedule is too busy	■ Rank your priorities. Make time for the important things.

■ What are some others? List them here and discuss them in your group now.

Obstacle	**What to Do About It**
_____	_____
_____	_____
_____	_____
_____	_____
_____	_____
_____	_____
_____	_____
_____	_____

Skills for Life

Congratulations! By completing this book, you have taken the first step to taking control of your life and accepting the responsibilities that go along with it.

Knowing what you can do and what you want to do, and how to do it is a big part of being successful in whatever you do.

This book about identifying your skills can help with the first step—the rest is up to you.

Good Luck!